ESL Writing Activities, Games +

Teaching Tips:

Practical Ideas for the Classroom

Jackie Bolen

(www.eslactivity.org)

Table of Contents

3

About the Author: Jackie Bolen

I taught English in South Korea for a decade to every level and type of student. I've taught every age from kindergarten kids to adults. Most of my time centered around teaching at two universities: five years at a science and engineering school out in the rice paddies of Chungcheongnam-Do, and four years at a major university in Busan where I taught high level classes for students majoring in English. I now teach ESL/EFL students in Vancouver, Canada. In my spare time, you can usually find me outside surfing, biking, hiking, or on the hunt for the most delicious kimchi I can find. It's not so easy in Vancouver!

In case you were wondering what my academic qualifications are, I hold a Master of Arts Degree in Psychology. During my time in Korea I successfully completed both the Cambridge CELTA and DELTA certification programs. With the combination of ten years teaching ESL/EFL learners of all ages and levels, and the more formal teaching qualifications I obtained, I have a solid foundation on which to offer teaching advice. I truly hope that you find this book useful and would love it if you sent me an email with any questions or feedback that you might have.

How did I get into teaching English writing? Well, I kind of fell into it when I moved from teaching young kids to university students. I taught ESL writing to beginners where we focused on making grammatically correct sentences. I also taught far more advanced students the ins and outs of academic writing. This involved five paragraph essays and preparing for the written portions of some of the popular English proficiency tests.

With time, I found that I liked teaching writing far more than I did conversation and speaking. As a result, I requested more of these classes from the administration at my university and they happily complied. Many teachers don't like to teach writing classes because of the heavier grading load compared to speaking classes. However, I always found it a nice change of pace and couldn't get enough of them.

The activities and games in this book are ones that I've used in my own classes and are tried and true! If you only teach beginners, there are also lots of activities for you. Teaching writing is about more than prepping students to write a five paragraph essay—which is all too often the primary focus of writing classes and courses. I also share my top tips for things like preventing cheating on writing exams, how to reduce the amount of time you spend on grading, and what students can actually write about. Let's get to it!

Jackie Bolen around the Internet

ESL Speaking (www.eslactivity.org)

Jackie Bolen (www.jackiebolen.com)

Twitter: @bolen_jackie

Email: jb.business.online@gmail.com

You may also want to check out some of other books on Amazon (search for Jackie Bolen), but here are a few of my most popular titles:

39 No-Prep/Low-Prep ESL Speaking Activities

39 Awesome 1-1 ESL Activities

101 ESL Activities for Teenagers and Adults

Life After ESL: Foreign Teachers Returning Home

Tips for Teaching ESL/EFL Writing

When it comes to teaching EFL/ESL writing, I believe that every teacher goes through a learning curve about how to teach different elements of writing no matter how good they personally are at writing let alone teaching the language skill. When I took the CELTA course, my tutor said that any time a student is writing English, it can be considered writing practice. Prior to this moment, however, I thought ESL writing was about teaching students how to write a paragraph or essay.

It's vital for teachers to avoid looking through the prism of 'I-must-teach-my-students-EVERYTHING-about-writing.' This will overwhelm you as well as diminish your teaching confidence and performance before you enter the classroom. My CELTA tutor's wisdom helped me to realize that when a student completes a simple writing task—things like filling in blanks correctly or learning how to write a basic sentence with SVO (subject verb object) in the right order—that these small and simple acts of writing are a good definition of successful learning and teaching practice for a teacher.

No matter what level your students are, they can benefit from some writing practice. Just be sure to meet them where they're at and choose games and activities according to this. Here are my top tips to help you out when teaching English writing to ESL or EFL students.

Tip #1: Student-Centred Teaching is ALWAYS Best

When you're teaching a language, whether speaking, writing, listening or reading, student-centred is always the way to go. What I mean by this is that students should be doing the work, not you! What exactly does this mean when teaching writing?

Students Improve by Spending More Time Writing and Reading

The best way to improve writing is to write and edit lots and also examine good examples of English writing! Design your classes so that students are getting as much practice as possible. There are more details in the last section of the book about what students can write about. However, here are a few quick ideas. Your students could write a journal entry in every class, do some editing, examine a piece of writing that uses a number of key elements well, or practice a specific writing skill like using conjunctions.

Reduce Lecture Time

How much are you talking and lecturing each class? Reduce this and get students to spend more time writing. In general (across all skills, not just writing), I try to lecture for less than five minutes for every thirty minutes of students doing a learning task.

Freedom for What to Write About

Whenever possible, students should have some degree of freedom to choose what they want to write about. For example, they can choose from among five different essay topics. Or, they are free to write an opinion essay about any topic as long as they check in with me first to make sure it's suitable.

Responsibility for Final Product is With the Students

Most importantly, you'll certainly want to avoid the trap of, "Teacher is responsible for correcting all errors in my writing." This is especially true if you want to have a life outside of teaching. Furthermore, you'll want to equip your students to go out into the real world where bosses aren't standing over your student's shoulder every time they have to send an important email to a client in English.

The Better Way: Self-Editing

The teacher being responsible for the final product is not ideal. What's the better way? Teaching self-editing. After all, isn't that what happens when your students have to write something at work? Or, take an English proficiency exam? It's certainly the better way so keep this in the back of your mind when designing your lessons and assigning homework.

Tip #2: Use a Grading Rubric for Evaluating Writing

For English teachers, grading writing and speaking are not easy when compared to something like grammar or vocabulary because there's often no right or wrong answer. Everything falls on a continuum from needs a lot of improvement to excellent.

The challenge for teachers is to grade in a way that's fair and that also appears this way to the students. To do this, you'll need an ESL writing rubric. I generally use the same one with all my writing classes and for a wide variety of topics. Of course, feel free to adapt it to suit your needs for each situation.

This ESL essay rubric started off more complicated but over the years I've simplified it. The best rubrics are simple enough that students can clearly understand why they received the grade that they did.

The Categories I Evaluate for English Writing

Each of these five categories has an equal number of possible points (from 0-5), for a total of 25 points. To make your grading life easier, if the essay is worth 30%, you can adjust the rubric to make each category out of six points. Or for 20%, make it out of four points.

If you make each section out of four points, you can use something like the following:

1 = inadequate

2 = needs improvement

3 = meets expectations

4 = exceeds expectations

Here are the categories that I look at when evaluating writing. I generally use the same one with all my writing classes and for a wide variety of topics.

1. sentences/paragraphs/format

2. grammar/spelling/punctuation/vocabulary

3. hook/thesis statement/topic sentences/ideas

4. task completion/effect on the reader

#1: Sentence Structure, Paragraphs, and Format

The best essays have sentences and paragraphs that are complete and easy to read. A nice variety of conjunctions and transitions are used to join them together.

#2: Grammar, Spelling, Punctuation, and Vocabulary

The best pieces of writing may only have 1-2 small errors in this area. There is a good use of higher level grammar and vocabulary.

This section includes pretty much all the formatting, language (vocabulary and grammar) that a student at their level would be expected to know, even if we explicitly haven't discussed it in class.

I will give my students a heads up about what I'm looking for. For example, if the essay topic lends itself to using the simple past and the students are intermediate or advanced, I'll mention that I expect their verbs to be perfect. I haven't explicitly taught this grammar point in my writing class, but it's something that students at this level should know cold, especially when writing because they have time to think about it and look it up if necessary.

Or, the writing piece may lend itself to lots of descriptive words (adjectives and adverbs). I'll mention to my higher-level students that I expect to see some interesting ones that are not the following: good, better, best, bad, beautiful, fun, nice, funny, slowly, quickly, etc.). Which ones they specifically use are up to them but my hope is that students push themselves a little bit with this and produce a piece of writing that is rich and alive.

#3: Hook, Thesis Statement, and Topic Sentence

To get full marks, all of these will have to be very well done. This is because I teach these things extensively in class and ensure that if students take away one thing from my writing course, it's how to do these things.

For things like reports, descriptive paragraphs, emails, etc., these components may not be found. However, there are other key pieces that will be needed to give structure and organization to the writing piece. I change this section to fit the writing style as needed.

#4: Ideas

The ideas in the writing are clear, logical and well organized. Good supporting facts and information are used. If it's a take-home assignment, I expect it to include real statistics and facts. If the essay is for a test written in class, then good logic will have to be used.

#5: Task Completion and Effect on the Reader

The best essays are easy to understand on a first, quick read-through. The student also followed the directions for the assignment (word count, etc.).

Show Students the Rubric When Explaining the Assignment

Something I try to be 100% clear about with my students whether it's a written assignment or a speaking test is how I'm going to evaluate it. In this case, when I'm explaining the assignment, I give students this rubric and go through it section by section to explain what I'm looking for. Students appreciate knowing what the expectations are and it'll save you a lot of time too because students will mostly understand why they got the grade that they did.

Can I Evaluate ESL/EFL Writing Without a Rubric?

You may be tempted to evaluate student writing without a rubric because you think it will save time. I don't recommend this unless you're teaching informally and the grades and feedback you give students don't count towards an official grade of some kind.

However, if you're teaching at a university in a credit class, grades matter and you need to have a reason for why you assigned the grade you did. Beyond that simple fact, here's why you should use a rubric to evaluate written work.

Writing rubrics help teachers and students in many ways. They save teachers huge amounts of time because students understand exactly how they got their grades. You will avoid a steady stream of students wanting to come to office hours and demand every deducted point be explained. A rubric helps students process the feedback and have a better idea about what specific writing skills need to improve. Lastly, if a student goes to your school admin and demands their grade be raised, you can show how and why a student got their grade if someone asks. When I taught in Korean universities there were a number of times when students challenged their scores or grades.

Can I Use This ESL Writing Grading Rubric for a Paragraph?

I used to teach academic writing to advanced students where they had to write five paragraph opinion essays. However, the rubric would work equally well for an opinion paragraph. In the case of using the rubric for an opinion paragraph, thesis and topic sentence become interchangeable: the first sentence should intro the topic as well as the opinion in an interesting way (hook). Sentence 2, 3, and 4 are supporting reasons, facts, and/or an example. Sentence 5 concludes the opinion/main idea. An opinion paragraph is essentially a mini-opinion essay. Many academic opinion essay books, especially for low level writing students, will have them learn how to write an opinion paragraph before moving on to the 5 paragraph opinion essay.

Tip #3: How Much Feedback to Give when Teaching Writing

It's an excellent question! When I teach English writing to intermediate or advanced level students, I'm ALL about teaching self-editing instead of having students rely on me to correct their errors. However, during the semester students are free to come to my office during my allotted hours to have a quick read-through of their writing. I'll usually give feedback along the lines of:

"Your thesis statement is kind of weak. Have a look at that and see if you can make it more concise."

11

"I noticed that you have very few transitions in your essay. It makes it kind of hard to read. Try adding in at least five of them"

"You have many grammar errors. For example, subject-verb agreement."

"Can you try to use some more complicated grammar or vocabulary? It's fine, but all the sentences are so similar and also quite simple."

"Pay closer attention to punctuation. For example, _____."

Beginners will require more personalized feedback from the teacher because they are usually not at the level where they are able to identify their own errors.

What about Feedback on Assignments and Tests?

Along with my grading rubric, I'll write some comments on my students' work, usually 3-4 sentences next to their grade. Throughout their essay, I'll also pick out around 5 things to circle as problems or errors.

I'll put a check mark as a sign of a good thing like the thesis statement or topic sentences.

Is it necessary to correct every single error? Not really. It's often more helpful to just point out mistakes that students have made more than once. That way, they have something solid to improve upon instead of just a whole bunch of seemingly unrelated mistakes.

Tip #4: Which ESL Writing Textbook Do you Recommend?

Are you looking for an excellent textbook for teaching academic writing to ESL or EFL students? Stop looking right now and go buy this: *Great Writing 4: From Great Paragraphs to Great Essays* by Keith Folse. You can easily find it on *Amazon*. Actually, this whole series is excellent from the first book to the last and you really don't need to consider any other!

The fourth book is an ideal introduction to writing an essay for high intermediate to advanced level English students. In my case, I used it when teaching 3rd or 4th year English majors at a university in South Korea.

Tip #5: How Do I Prevent Cheating in a Writing Class?

If you teach writing in a for-credit class where you have to assign grades, you will almost certainly have students who try to cheat. There are a few things that I do to combat this and make things fair for the students.

Homework Assignments are Not Worth that Many Marks

During my writing courses, I do give homework assignments. They just aren't worth that many points. For example, the maximum is 20% of the final grade (usually four assignments worth 5% each).

The bulk of the grade is things we do in class: journaling and then the midterm and final exams that have to be physically written in my classroom. This gives me a better indication of who can write well without having an Internet crutch to assist them.

The Ultimate Thing to Do on the First Day of Writing Class

On the first day of any writing class, I get students to complete a "Get to know you assignment." I give them about 20 minutes to write three short paragraphs that include the following:

- the past (high school days, growing up, etc.)

- the present (university life and their thoughts about it)

- the future (dreams, hopes, etc.)

This shows how proficient students are at the past/present/future verb tenses and it's often quite obvious who will do well in your class and who will likely struggle.

Then, keep these papers and in case of a questionable homework assignment, you have something to compare it to. For example, I had one student submit something that I

13

myself probably couldn't have produced. It was that good and had advanced level vocabulary that I had to look up to find out the meanings to. Plus, there wasn't a single grammatical error in the whole assignment, which is certainly quite unusual for someone who doesn't speak English as their first language. It's even unusual for someone who does!

I pulled out her assignment from the first day and found it riddled with simple mistakes like not using the correct past tense verb form and other similar mistakes. She clearly could not have done that homework assignment herself and my guess is that she paid someone to do it because I was unable to find it through a Google search.

Of course, for some other students I'm able to find their work using Google which makes it easier to deal with.

Midterm/Final Exam: Assign Random Topics

Some teachers assign a single topic for their exams and then allow the students to prepare their essay beforehand. During the exam, they just have to write it out. I try to avoid this.

Instead, I give students a list of around 20 possible topics. Then, I give students a slip of paper with two possible choices that they must choose from. Each student gets a random combination or two choices so there is no chance to copy off a neighbor.

This allows students to prepare for the exam in terms of ideas and main points, but they can't memorize an essay word for word. I find it to be a better test of writing ability and there's clearly no way to cheat on this kind of exam.

Tip #6: All About Teaching Writing to ESL Beginners

Teaching beginners to write in English can be a very difficult job. These students often struggle to put together a sentence, so teaching them to "write" can be quite overwhelming. Many teachers instead find themselves just focusing on students' grammar mistakes. This isn't a terrible thing, but then it kind of becomes a grammar class instead of one focused on

14

writing. Here's how to avoid this problem.

Use this Writing Activity for Lower Level Students

Take whatever topic you're studying in the unit. For example, free time leisure activities. Then, make a fill in the blank paragraph on the board or PowerPoint for the students to copy.

I live in _____. In _____, people like to _____, _____, _____ and _____ in their free time. Young people think _____ is _____ because _____.

First, I fill in the blanks using the city where my university is (and where I happen to live) and I get the students to help me. Then, I turn the students loose to do their own hometown, which takes about 5 minutes for something as simple as this. My hope is that the students can get the hang of making some interesting, grammatically correct sentences and still use some of their own creativity and thinking power.

Keep going, leaving out more and more blanks for students to fill in as they get better with it. Eventually, you may just have a couple of words to start off each sentence and they can complete it.

Example-1st, Production-2nd

For beginners, it really is about examples first and production second so help your students out by giving them something solid to grasp. Most beginning students can partially copy what's on the board and then adapt it to make it true for them. This isn't a bad thing if that's where students are at in terms of ability.

The Worst Thing to Do with Beginner Students and Writing

If you have beginner students, don't make this same mistake that many of my colleagues seem to do. They give a homework assignment that consists of something like, "Write a movie review" or, "Write a short essay about XYZ."

15

Then, they get back page after page of gibberish that was obviously cut and pasted from a translator program. Or, they get something perfect that was cut and pasted from Wikipedia.

It's far better to give students an extremely specific question that they won't be able to copy. For example, "What are three things our university administration could change to make it better?" or, "What are three things you have learned in this class?" Specific instead of general is the way to go if you're going to give this kind of assignment.

Use this Beginner Writing Textbook

If you're teaching an intensive writing class (and not just doing writing as part of a 4-skills class) and are looking for a beginner level ESL writing textbook for high school students or adults, my top recommendation is *Great Writing 1: Great Sentences for Great Paragraphs* by Keith Folse (easily found on *Amazon*). It focuses on the sentence and paragraph level, which will be challenging enough for beginner English students.

Trust me, there are lots of books out there but none are better than this one if you want to focus specifically on writing. It has a nice blend of process and product approaches to teaching writing. Students learn how to do things like editing, use varied vocabulary, etc. They also study the finished product and have to replicate it for themselves.

Tip #7: How Can I Foster Student Autonomy in Writing Classes?

Autonomy, with regards to teaching, is when students take charge of their own learning. That is, they are responsible for it and the teacher is more of a guide than the all-knowing one who imparts wisdom and knowledge.

Teacher as Editor Model: Bad News!

I believe that the current model of teaching writing in most universities in Korea (and perhaps around the world where English is taught as a second or foreign language) does nothing to foster student autonomy. When I attend conferences, I hear people giving presentations about teaching writing without even a mention of self-editing, instead focusing on teacher, or peer-editing, exclusively.

This model of teacher editor is basically where the student writes something and gives it to the teacher, probably with very little in the way of self-editing, if any at all.

In fact, it's not so uncommon that the student (especially at lower-levels) will give something to the teacher that came straight from Google Translate. Then the teacher spends ridiculous amounts of time editing something that in some cases is barely understandable and gives it back to the student. They make the necessary changes, often mindlessly, and don't really look at the mistakes in detail. And then hand it in to the teacher again.

This cycle can repeat endlessly without the student improving their writing!

Peer as Editor: Bad News Also!

This same cycle can also be done with peer editing, which I am not a big fan of either. In both of these models, the learner essentially takes very little responsibility for turning out a quality product on their own because they know that the teacher or friend will just make the changes they need.

However, peer or teacher editing is 100% unlike real life. When students are taking an English proficiency test that involves writing, there is no teacher or friend sitting next to them, helping them along. Nor would they have this at any job. They would just be expected to turn out a decent email or essay or whatever else they would need to write by themselves.

How about Teaching Self-Editing Instead?

In an attempt to foster student autonomy by teaching writing strategies, I teach students to self-edit by giving them check-lists with things like:

1. Check all the verbs: correct tense?

2. What is your thesis statement? Circle it! Is it stated or implied? Underline the topic sentences. Put a box around your restated thesis.

3. Does each sentence have a capital letter and period/question mark/exclamation point? Circle them.

Tip #8: Include Writing in Speaking and Conversation Classes

Just because you teach a conversation class doesn't mean that you shouldn't throw a little bit of writing practice in there too! Why should you consider doing this? Here are a few important reasons.

First of all, some students are introverted. I'm a bit of an introvert myself and nothing makes me more tired than a class full of upbeat and cheery conversation activities. That's why I like to incorporate some quieter, individual work into each lesson. A short writing exercise or activity of some kind based on the topic of the day is ideal for this.

Secondly, nothing solidifies grammar or vocabulary more solidly than writing it down on a piece of paper. I think it's sometimes the case where we teach something and students practice it by speaking, but then it never really gets to the next level of actually "knowing" it. Writing can help our students get there, and it also gives you the chance to offer some very specific feedback to every single student, which often isn't the case in bigger speaking classes.

Finally, English writing is an important skill that many students don't feel confident with because they don't practice it enough. At least in South Korea where I taught for many years, it'd be normal for English majors to take 10+ speaking or conversation courses, but only 1-2 writing courses. That's why in those speaking ones, I tried to incorporate a little bit of writing. Think about the big picture for your students and whether or not they need more writing practice. If they do, maybe you can be the one to give it to them!

Tip #9: Reasoning and Critical Thinking are Also Important

When you're teaching someone how to write an essay, it's easy to get bogged down with thesis statements, hooks, topic sentences, and using correct grammar and vocabulary. However, don't forget about the importance of what students are actually writing about. By this, I mean their ideas and opinions and then the facts, reasons and examples they use to support them.

Teach your students how to brainstorm ideas and then choose the strongest ones. This is the perfect activity to do in small groups of 3-4 students. It's important enough that you may want to spend an entire class or two on this! If you use the *Great Writing Series* by Keith Folse, there are some excellent sections related to this that I found extremely helpful.

Tip #10: Teach the Writing Process

Most teachers probably already know this from their university days, but it can be helpful to see it written out! When writing, use the writing process. Your students can use this for just about anything.

Step 1: Pre-writing — Think about what you're going to write. Brainstorm some ideas. Choose the best ideas and make an outline. The outline can be very simple, or very detailed. It depends on you. However, don't write full sentence in the outline. Only make a few notes.

Step 2: Writing — Take your ideas and make them into sentences and paragraphs. Don't worry about if it's good, or not. Your first draft will almost always be terrible!

Step 3: Editing — Read what you've written slowly and carefully. Does it make sense? Are there any errors. You can repeat steps two and three as often as necessary.

Step 4: Formatting the Final Product — This step involves getting it ready for whatever you're using it for. It may be handing it in to a teacher, uploading it on a blog, or entering an essay competition. Whatever the case, there are usually expectations for what the final product should look like.

Tip #11: All About Writing Style

I certainly know that English teachers have differing opinions about academic writing style rules and formats. However, my personal preference is that students write simply and concisely with few errors. I much prefer simple vocabulary and grammatical constructions as opposed to lots of very long sentences with all kinds of conjunctions and clauses.

Why? Think about the reader. There's almost no situation in life that calls for extremely advanced level writing —except for an academic journal where you'd be judged poorly for communicating your points clearly and easily. No reader should have to go back through your paragraph 2-3 times just to understand the gist of it. Even an academic journal could probably benefit from making its writing more reader-friendly!

Now, consider students who are writing in English (which isn't their first language). This can compound the problem of not getting the point across clearly because there will be grammatical errors and strange vocabulary choices.

If my students can use sentences that are almost perfect, anyone who is reading should be able to understand what they mean quickly and without having to read it again. What about long, complicated sentences that are filled with errors? It'll likely be far more difficult for the reader to understand the intended meaning, unless the student is quite advanced and able to do this almost perfectly.

Use your own judgement on this, but I will always err on the side of simplicity! Here's the advice that I give my students.

Write Concisely

When writing in some languages such as Korean, the longer the sentences the better! Sentences are very complicated and sometimes even quite difficult for a native speaker to fully understand them. When students try to translate these sentence directly into English, the results are often not good!

Simple English can be beautiful. It doesn't require long, complicated sentences. It's usually better to write concisely and say what you need to in as few words as possible. This is especially true for beginners. It's better to make short, simple, but perfect sentences rather than long, complicated sentences with many grammatical errors. Think simple. Think short. This will help readers be able to understand the writing quickly and easily.

Tip #12: Mistakes are Unavoidable

Mistakes are unavoidable. Some students are very hard on themselves when learning to write, especially when it comes to feedback. Here's the advice that I give my students in writing classes.

When learning something new, it's normal to make a lot of mistakes. This is a fact! This applies to anything and not just English! Remember cooking for the first time? It probably wasn't so delicious and took a really long time. The kitchen was likely a disaster too. How about the first time shooting a basketball? It probably didn't go in!

Learning a language is the same. Nobody is good when they start but the key is to keep practicing and getting better. Fear of making mistakes is normal, but it's not helpful. The key is to overcome this and just write. Of course, lots of mistakes will happen, however the most important thing is to keep trying.

Have a Positive Attitude about Criticism

The people who are best at English are those that have a positive attitude about criticism. When a teacher or peer gives them feedback about something they wrote, they love it! These people also regularly seek out feedback, and are willing to get it from just about anyone. They realize that they can learn something from a lot of different people. Basically, they want everyone to read their writing and aren't shy about asking!

On the other hand, people who aren't good at English are really shy about sharing their writing with other people. They often feel embarrassed by their lack of writing skill. However, asking for feedback isn't a sign of weakness. Teachers love it when students ask for help! The best students share their writing with lots of people and welcome any ideas that other people have about it.

Writing Activities for All Levels

Here are some of my favourite writing activities that can be used with any level of student.

3 Things

Skills: Writing/listening

Time: 10+ minutes

Level: Beginner-advanced

Materials Required: Nothing

Have students think of three random things for a partner. For example: A, B, and C. They should be objects, animals or people of some kind.

Then, students have to write a story using all three of these things. It can be silly, and actually, the sillier the better! The length of the story and the time you give depends on the level of your students. Students can share their story with the person who thought of the three objects.

For beginners, you may want to do this together as a class. The students could shout out three random words and then you can write them on the board. Then, they could help you write a simple story using those words. Or, you may want to consider showing them an example of a simple, silly story using random words and then have them make their own using new words but with many of the same sentences from the example one.

Procedure:

1. Put students into pairs and each person has to think of three random objects for their partner.

2. Students have to write a short story using those three objects. Consider using an adaptation (mentioned above) for beginners.

3. Then, they can share their story with their partner. You can also ask for volunteers to share their stories with the class or require that students turn in a more polished version of this for a homework assignment.

Conjunctions and Transitions: Don't Forget About Them

Skills: Writing

Time: Variable

Level: Beginner-advanced

Materials Required: Conjunction and transition worksheets

When teaching writing to English learners, it's sometimes easy to get overwhelmed when considering the big picture. How do you teach someone to write grammatically correct sentences if each sentence they write has multiple mistakes in it? Or, teach someone who has a difficult time at the sentence level to write an essay?

One of the keys to not getting overwhelmed is to focus on one thing at a time. For example, conjunctions and transitions. They're very important in English writing and certainly worth doing a lesson on them with any level of students. Here's a bit more information about them for students who may know about these things in their first language but not know the English words associated with them.

Conjunctions and transitions are important for letting readers know how sentences and paragraphs are connected. Conjunctions and transitions join clauses, sentences, and paragraphs.

There are four types of conjunctions: coordinating, correlative, subordinating, and adverbial/linking conjunctions. You probably learned FANBOYS to remember coordinating conjunctions: F: for, A: and, N: nor, B: but, O: or, Y: yet, and S: so. These words can join nouns, pronouns, verbs, adjectives, adverbs, phrases, and clauses. These come in quite handy when a student wants to merge short sentences in order to make longer ones.

Correlative conjunctions are pairs of words used to emphasize the relationship between two items. Note: the items can be nouns, verbs, adjectives, or adverbs, but both parts must be the same.

The five correlative conjunctions are:

both _____ and _____

not _____ and _____

either _____ or _____

neither _____ nor _____

not only _____ but also _____

Subordinating conjunctions are used to create subordinate clauses which must be paired with a main clause to make a complete sentence. These words include: after, although, as, as much as, because, before, how, if, in order that, since, than, that, unless, and until.

Finally, linking adverbs, like coordinating conjunctions, join two sentences. The difference is that they show more types of relationships between the two clauses: continuation, contrast, sequence, cause and effect, and result. You can show continuation with these words: also, beside, further, furthermore, in addition, and moreover. For example, you can show contrast with these words: conversely, however, instead, nevertheless, nonetheless, and on the other hand.

Transitions can be used to show addition, comparison, contrast, summary, condition, cause and effect/result, or time/sequence. Additive transitions are used when adding similar ideas or information. Comparative transitions show similarities, while adversative transitions are used to introduce ideas which contrast with or do not agree with the previous ones. Causal transitions show cause and effect or reason and result. Sequential transitions show the chronological (time) or logical order. Other transitional words and phrases indicate some condition, such as: whether, otherwise, and however+adverb. Others can summarize previous statements, such as: finally, in other words, and therefore.

How Can I Get My Students to Practice Them?

That's an excellent question! There are a number of ways that you can get your students working on these. For beginners, you may want to start with a worksheet or two to get them choosing the correct one for the situation. Or, go through a piece of writing and circle all the ones they can find.

For more advanced writers, they can use something they've written and then add in a few of these words to improve their writing. The number that you'd want them to add depends on the length of the writing passage.

Some of my favourite places to find worksheets include the following:

- *Teachers Pay Teachers* (https://www.teacherspayteachers.com/)

- *ESL Flow* (https://eslflow.com/)

- *Agenda Web* (https://agendaweb.org/)

- *ISL Collective* (https://en.islcollective.com/)

Dictation Practice

Skills: Writing/listening

Time: 5-10 minutes

Level: Beginner-advanced

Materials Required: A text to dictate

Dictation is an excellent way for your students to practice their listening and writing skills. It helps students practice a range of sub-skills from printing English letters to punctuation, spelling, proof-reading and lay-out. Dictation can also offer a serious dose of syntax, vocabulary and grammar! In short, it's an extremely versatile activity and a nice break from the very communicative activities that dominate most of our textbooks and classes today.

The way it works is that you find a writing passage that you'll read to your students. Or, you could even make up your own on the fly for a truly no-prep activity. In an emergency situation, just grab something off the shelf in the teacher's office or from your desk and it should work in most cases.

However, if you have a wee bit more time, some good sources for writing passages are the textbook you're using for the class, a website like *Breaking News English*, or just about anything for that matter! You may even want to write it yourself. The key is finding something at a similar level to your students, or just slightly below.

Read out the passage to your students who write down what they hear. You may have to read it again, depending on the level of your students. I generally give students a minute or two at the end for proofreading and instruct them to check things like spelling and punctuation. Check answers and correct any errors with spelling, punctuation, etc. Or, you can write the passage on the board or online and students can check their own answers.

Procedure:

1. Choose a passage that you'll read to your students.

2. Read the passage and students have to write down what they hear.

3. Give students some time for proofreading and then optionally, they can compare with a partner.

4. Finally, the teacher can check students' answers by walking around the class. Or, they can submit it for marking outside of class. If you have a class website, you can post the original version there after class and students can check their own work.

Picture Prompt

Skills: Writing

Time: 5 minutes

Level: Beginner-advanced

Materials Required: A picture with people doing things

Picture prompt is a great ESL warm-up for kids as well as adults. It can be used for all levels from beginner to advanced. Show students an image and have them generate questions or speculate about the picture. In this case, you'd want to do it with writing, although this activity lends itself to speaking as well. In particular, it works well if you're teaching your students about questions forms, transitions, relative clauses or adjectives.

Question Examples for Beginner Students

For lower level students, this can be purely descriptive:

Q: What do you see?

A: I see a house, a car, and some people.

Q: What colour is the car?

A: It is blue.

Question Examples for Intermediate Level Students

For high beginner/low intermediate students, have an image which can generate questions such as:

What is happening in this picture?

27

How does that person feel?

Why do you think so?

Or, you may also use it to focus on English prepositions. For example:

Where is the book?

Is the man standing next to the child?

Example Questions for Advanced Students

For more advanced students, use an unusual image. Encourage them to create a narrative to explain the story. You could have students create a story about the picture in a few minutes. Or, you could have them write an explanation for what happened.

Teaching Tips:

You can find collections of unusual images online which are perfect for advanced students to create their narratives. Just search on Google Images or something similar according to your topic that day.

For beginners, you can either say the questions out loud and students have to answer them, or you could make a worksheet with room for students' answers.

If you have more advanced students in a writing class, more options are available to you for what you can do. You may even require students to write a paragraph, essay or a creative story based on the picture that you show them.

Procedure:

1. In advance, prepare an image, either PowerPoint or a picture large enough for the class to easily see.

2. Divide students into pairs or small groups (optional).

3. Depending on the level of the students and the focus of your lesson you may do the following:

A. Elicit descriptive sentences about the image. Encourage them to make their own questions to ask a partner.

B. Have them write down what they think is happening in the picture, how the person/people feel and why they think so, etc.

C. Have them create a narrative about the image. (Unusual images work well for this.)

Complete a worksheet of simple questions.

Postcards

Skills: Writing/reading

Time: 15+ minutes

Level: Beginner-advanced

Materials Required: Postcards

If you can get your hands on some cheap postcards or have some laying around your house or teacher's office, try out this fun writing activity. It may just be the novelty factor, but students seem to love it. This activity is ideal for working on common greetings, the past tense, using descriptive words, as well as using synonyms to avoid repetition.

Distribute the postcards to the students. You can do one per student, or put the students into pairs. They have to look at the picture on the front of the postcard and imagine that they went on this vacation. Then, they can write about their trip to a friend or family member.

Next, the students trade postcards with another student or group. After reading them, they can write a response back of at least a few sentences. Finally, you may want to display them around the class as they're colorful and fun and other students may enjoy reading them!

Procedure:

1. Give each student or pair a postcard. They look at the picture and imagine what they did on that vacation, and then pretend that they're writing to a friend or family member.

2. Exchange postcards and another student or group has to write a response to what they read.

3. Display the postcards around your classroom (optional).

Practice Writing Fluently

Skills: Writing

Time: 5-10 minutes/class

Level: High beginner-advanced

Materials Required: Notebook

For speaking and writing, there are two main ways to evaluate it: fluency and accuracy. Fluency is how fast you are able to do it. Accuracy is how good your grammar and vocabulary are. It's more complicated than that, but that's the simple explanation!

Most English writing classes and textbooks focus on accuracy. It's much easier for a book, or teacher to point out grammar and vocab errors than to teach you to write quickly. However, it's important to work on both. The good news is that you can easily help your students with writing fluency.

Each student needs a notebook that they'll use only for this purpose. Assign students a topic for each class they will do the fluency writing practice in. For example, "My family," or, "Plans for the weekend," or, "Hopes for the future," or, "My favourite book." Then, have them write about that topic for five minutes (or ten once they get used to it) without using a cellphone and dictionary. Beginners may only be able to do it for three minutes. The goal is to write quickly. If students don't know how to spell something, just guess. It doesn't matter in a fluency writing exercise.

This is the most important thing—the pen should NEVER stop moving. If they can't think of anything, write this sentence, "I don't know what to write. I don't know what to write. I don't. . ." After two or three times, they'll think of something else! If you see a student not writing, tell them to make sure that their pen doesn't stop moving.

Over time, you'll notice that the amount they can write increases! Remember that the goal is to write more quickly, not to write accurately. Your students can work on grammar, vocabulary and structure at other times.

Procedure:

1. Students get a notebook specifically for fluent writing practice.

2. Assign a topic of the day and amount of time to write.

3. Students write for that specified amount of time without a cell-phone or dictionary. The goal is to write quickly.

4. Pens should never stop moving! Students can write, "I don't know what to write" instead.

5. Track progress over time with a word count chart.

Proofreading Practice

Skills: Writing/reading

Time: 5-10 minutes

Level: Beginner-advanced

Materials Required: Worksheet with errors

How you design this activity will vary greatly depending on the level of your students. Beginner level students can generally only proofread 1-3 things when they start developing self-editing skills. For example, tell them to check that the first word of each sentence is capitalized and has a period at the end. Advanced level students can handle a wide range of errors that include punctuation, spelling, grammar, vocabulary, flawed logic and more.

Not proofreading writing is the biggest writing mistake. This applies to students who are studying English as a second or third language, as well as native speakers. Here's the advice that I give my students about this important topic.

After you write, allow yourself some time to read your work. If you're doing a writing test that is one hour long, I recommend the following:

1. 5 minutes planning. Write a few notes. Make a plan. What is your first, second, and third main point (if writing an essay)?

2. 45-50 minutes writing.

3. 5-10 minutes proofreading. Check writing for any mistakes. I recommend double-spacing, so it's easy to make any changes if you need to. Cross off what you wrote and then write in the line above it.

Reading out loud each and every single word is a good habit to get into. Pay close attention to things like subject-verb agreement (He is, She goes), spelling, capital letters, punctuation, etc.

If students do only one thing to improve their writing, it's this! ALWAYS proofread. Always! Here's a proofreading checklist I made for my university students in South Korea that you may want to consider using with yours: www.jackiebolen.com/proofreading.

Procedure:

1. Explain to your students about proofreading and give them a checklist for things to check.

2. Prepare a worksheet of sentences, a paragraph or an essay (depending on the level) that has some errors from the checklist on it.

3. Students have to go through the worksheet finding the errors. Check answers together as a class.

Word of the Day

Skills: Writing

Time: 5 minutes

Level: Beginner-advanced

Materials Required: Whiteboard/PowerPoint

I have frequently been required to either give my students a word, quote, or idiom of the day, outside of our usual textbook, but it's usually related to the textbook or a monthly theme. You can easily start a Word of the Day activity for your students, by giving them a single word each day from their textbook (but not a vocabulary word), current events or by having a theme for each month.

Write the word on the whiteboard or PowerPoint along with the definition, part of speech, and several example sentences. Have students copy all of this in their notebooks in a section for their Words of the Day. You can use the word as an exit ticket, have a weekly quiz, or add one or two words to each regular vocabulary quiz.

Variation (more advanced): Idiom of the Day is where you give students an idiom with a definition and a picture (if possible). Have them make 1-3 sentences using it correctly.

Procedure:

1. In advance, prepare a collection of words from your students' textbook but not part of the vocabulary list.

2. Begin each day (or one day per week) with one new word. Introduce the word just as you would their regular vocabulary: present the word, the definition, part of speech and several example sentences.

3. Have students copy the sentences in the notebooks and add their own sentence.

4. Add all or some Words of the Day to your regular vocabulary quizzes.

Words in Words

Skills: Writing

Time: 5-10 minutes

Level: Beginner-advanced

You probably did this when you were in school. Give students a word and have them make as many words as possible using the letters in that word. For example: "vacation" = a, on, no, act, action, taco, ant, van, etc. You can give a point for each word, so that the student with the most words wins, or give more points for longer words. When time is up (about five minutes), show students the possible answers.

Wordles.com has a tool that allows you to type in a word and get the possible words. For vacation, they listed 45 words, some of which I should have thought of myself and some of which are "Scrabble words." Since your students will not possibly know all of these words, it is up to you whether you show all the answers or an abridged list.

Procedure:

1. In advance, prepare a long word and write it on the whiteboard or a PowerPoint or give students individual worksheets.

2. Give students a time limit of about five minutes to make words from the letters in the word.

3. To make it a competition, when time is up, you can give students points for each word and you may wish to give bonus points for longer words.

4. When the activity is finished, show students all of the possible words they could have made. You can get these from *www.wordles.com.*

Writing Activities for Upper-Level Students

Check out some of my favourite writing activities for more advanced students.

5 Senses

Skills: Writing

Time: 5 minutes/round

Level: Intermediate-advanced

Materials Required: An object(s)

This activity is a fun way to help students work on descriptive writing. Bring in an object to class like a piece of chocolate or a carrot. It should be something that you can eat in order to do the "taste" sense. In groups, students have to write down a few descriptive words for each sense (see, smell, feel, hear, taste). Obviously, "hear" will not be easy for a carrot, but you could tell students to think about what happens when you snap a carrot in half.

When the time is up, each group can share 2-3 of their most interesting words with the class. You can also do this activity with another object if you wish. It works well as a daily warm-up in a writing class, if you bring in something different each day.

Procedure:

1. Bring an object to class that you can eat or drink.

2. Put students into small groups and they have to think of a few words for each of the senses related to that object (see, smell, feel, hear, taste).

3. At the end of the allotted time, each group can share a few of their most interesting words with the class.

4. Do another round with a different object if you'd like. Or, make it a regular warmer activity.

Association

Skills: Writing/reading/listening

Time: 20+ minutes

Level: Intermediate-advanced

Materials Required: List of words related to a theme

A fun way to get students writing is this "association game." Think of a number of words related to a certain theme. For example, the theme of travel could use the following words: holidays, relax, vacation, transportation, food, etc.

You can say these words one by one and students have to write down the first word that comes to mind when you say it. Using the list from above, they might write: Thailand, beach, fun, motorcycle, curry.

When this is done, students can write a story using the words they've thought of. It may or may not be a true story, but it doesn't really matter either way. To make it more fun, I require that students must use every word they wrote down once! Of course, allow some time for proofreading and editing before sharing the story with other students.

At the end, you can have students share their stories with another student (larger classes), or with everyone for smaller classes.

Procedure:

1. Think of at least 5-10 words related to a certain theme or topic.

2. Say the words one by one and students have to write down the first word that comes to mind.

3. Using these words, students have to write a story. It can be true or not true. Finally, have students share their story with another student or with the class.

Boggle

Skills: Writing

Time: 10 minutes

Level: Intermediate-advanced

You've probably played the word game Boggle before. You shake up the letters and then you have a certain amount of time to make some words with connecting letters. You can play it with your students but you don't need the actual Boggle game.

Simply make up a grid on the whiteboard, PowerPoint or on a piece of paper. It only takes a minute to do this. I make a 6x6 grid and put some obvious words in like the names of colors or animals, or the vocabulary that we've recently been studying. Then, students divide into pairs and they have to make as many words as possible that are 4+ letters. You can give a bonus for longer words if you like. For example, they get two points instead of one if their word is six letters or more.

A quick tip to point out to your students is to make good use of the "S." They can essentially get two words instead of one by using it. For example:

– fire, fires, mane, manes, fate, fates

This will help the groups who figure this out from running away with the game when other groups have not!

At the end, students count up how many points they have. You can double-check for any errors and then award a small prize to the winning team. Depending on class size and how much time you have, you can check the answers of the top 1-2 teams or all of them.

Procedure:

1. Prepare a "Boggle" grid. The no preparation way is to draw it on the whiteboard.

2. Students divide into pairs and try to make as many words as possible with 4+ letters.

Students cannot use/repeat the same letter in a single square within a single word.

3. Students add up points. The teacher checks the answers of all the teams, or only the top teams who will get a prize.

o	r	p	t	s	a
e	a	i	e	t	f
b	k	n	e	r	i
a	d	r	g	o	r
c	o	t	l	s	e
k	f	h	m	a	n

Some possible words from this board:

green, pink, rake, back, fire, fires, fast, road, rose, mane, manes (there are many others)

Bucket Lists

Skills: Writing

Time: 5-10 minutes

Level: Intermediate-advanced

Write a sample bucket list on the whiteboard and do a demonstration of how to talk about a bucket list. Give students about five minutes to create a list of three things they want to do, see, or accomplish before they die. Have them partner up to discuss their three wishes for 2-3 minutes, then change partners.

Procedure:

1. Begin by asking students if they have heard the term "bucket list." Then, show them your written example on the whiteboard of three things you want to do, see, or accomplish before you die.

2. Give students about five minutes to create their own bucket lists.

3. Divide students into partners to share their bucket lists, then have them change partners. Encourage the students to ask each other some follow-up questions about the list.

Fill out an Application Form

Skills: Reading/writing

Time: 20+ minutes

Level: Intermediate-advanced

Materials Required: Application form

During a teacher training course, my tutor mentioned that "writing" is not only writing essays. He said that we can get our students to practice writing just about anything and it would be useful. That comment changed my outlook on teaching writing, especially to beginners.

One simple thing that beginners can do is fill out an application form for a job. To find an application form, Google "sample job application form USA." Here's one example: http://www.careerchoices.com/lounge/files/jobapplication.pdf. Filling out an application form is a very practical activity. People have to fill them when they want to get a job, visa, or for traveling.

Procedure

1. Print off some application forms from the Internet.

2. Teach some application form vocabulary that you anticipate your students will have problems with, as well as tips for answering some questions.

3. Students fill out the application forms while you circulate and offer some feedback.

Freeze

Skills: Writing/reading/listening

Time: 5-20 minutes

Level: Intermediate-advanced

Materials Required: Nothing

This is a group writing activity that you can have a lot of fun with. The way it works is that you think of a story starter. For example, "Tom decided to _____." Students have to start the story off, and after 30 seconds or a minute, you can say, "Freeze."

Then, students pass their paper one to the right/behind/etc., depending on how the classroom is arranged. That student has to read the story and then continue it. You can repeat the freeze and pass as many times as you like, but I usually give a warning when it's the last round so students can finish up the story.

Read the stories out loud to the class and see which one is the best.

Procedure:

1. Write a story starter on the board. For example, "Amy had a terrible day! She _____."

2. Each student has to continue the story for 30 seconds to 1 minute. Then say, "Freeze!"

3. Students pass their paper in an organized fashion and continue the story. Repeat as many times as you like, but warn students when it's the last round so they can finish it off.

4. Read the stories out loud with the class.

Movie Subtitles

Skill: Writing

Time: 10-30 minutes

Level: Intermediate-advanced

Materials Required: Short film or movie clip

Who doesn't like watching movies, right? Try out this fun activity that gets your students making up subtitles for a short film or part of a movie or TV show. Find an interesting clip on *YouTube*. You'll want something with action and speaking, but not too much or it can be too difficult. It's easiest with only two people. Or, one person talking to themselves.

Show the clip for a few seconds with the volume turned off and have students work in pairs or small groups to make subtitles for what the people are saying. When everyone is ready, play a few more seconds and students can write the subtitles for the next short exchange by the characters. You should mark the timing of this as you do it on a piece of paper.

At the end, have each group come to the front and read out their subtitles as you play through the clip. If there are two people talking in your film, have one group member play each person.

Procedure:

1. Choose a short movie clip with some dialogue.

2. Play a few seconds with the volume off and students can work in pairs or small groups to make subtitles for what the people are saying. Play a few more seconds and continue on as long as you'd like. Allow for some proofreading and tidying up time at the end of this. I prefer having students do this on their own work because it replicates real life better than peer-editing or teacher-editing does. I do make myself available for questions or assistance during this time.

3. When done, each group can have a chance to share what they wrote with the class as you play through the clip.

Only 1 Question

Skills: Listening/speaking/writing

Time: 15-20 minutes

Level: Intermediate-advanced

Materials Required: Pen, paper

This activity gets students working on question forms, taking notes as well as summarizing and reporting results. Students have to think of one question about a topic and write it down. For example, if you're studying about holidays, they could use any of the following:

"What's your least favorite holiday?"

"What did you do last _____?"

"What do you think about Valentine's Day?"

There are many possibilities but I usually make a couple rules that it must be interesting and also that it can't be a yes/no question. Once students have done this, they ask at least ten people their question and quickly record their answers with just a few words.

After the time is up, they tabulate the answers and can quickly report to a small group what they found out about the topic. You can ask each small group to share the most interesting thing they learned with the entire class.

Procedure:

1. Give students a topic and have each student make one *interesting* question about it. Give them examples of interesting versus boring questions.

2. Each student talks to at least ten students, using the same question. They quickly write down answers with a few words.

3. Students tabulate the results, write down their findings and report them to a small group of

4-6 people (or the entire class if fewer than 10 students). For homework, you could have students submit a short report of their findings.

Plan a Trip

Skills: Writing

Time: 20+ minutes

Level: Intermediate-advanced

Materials Required: Information from the Internet

      Have your students plan a dream vacation in English! Instead of researching in their first language, use *Google* in English. In order to practice writing, keep notes only in English. Here's an example of how you might plan your trip using English. You can have your students add as little, or as much detail as you'd like. However, the point of the activity is to practice writing in point form which is useful when writing outlines for tests or essays.

Day 1: Monday, January 1

Fly Seoul (3pm) ----> Vancouver (7am)

Check in Hotel ABC, 123 Avenue

Rest, relax

Day 2: Tuesday, January 2

Stay Hotel ABC

Tour Stanley Park

Eat Pub XYZ dinner

Day 3: Wednesday, January 3

Check out Hotel ABC

Rent car Budget 123

Drive Whistler

Rent skis shop ABC

Go Skiing

Lunch ski lodge

Check in Hotel ABC Whistler

Bed early

Procedure:

1.Give students time to do some Internet research about a place they want to go. It's helpful to specify the number of days. I generally make a rule that they must do this research in English. Suggest some helpful websites where they might like to start (*Trip Advisor, Air BnB*, etc.).

2. Students can make a day-by-day itinerary of what they're trip is going to look like.

3. They can share about their trip with the class or turn it in for a graded assignment.

Paraphrasing Practice

Skills: Reading/writing

Time: Variable

Level: Intermediate-advanced

Materials Required: Passage to paraphrase (lecture, newspaper article, etc.)

Paraphrasing is an important writing skill. If your students are planning to take a test such as the TOEFL, TOEIC, or IELTS, they will need to be able to paraphrase effectively. Paraphrasing uses your words to state the main points of a text without adding any information, such as your opinion or previous knowledge of the topic.

To help your students practice paraphrasing, choose a short newspaper article. They can begin by circling words which cannot be changed: places, names, dates, etc. Then, they can see if any information can be combined or rearranged. Next, they could consider the best synonyms to replace the nouns, verbs, and adjectives. Finally, they can reread the original text and compare it with your paraphrase. Do both texts have the same meaning? If not, keep trying.

Procedure

1. Give students a passage that they can read.

2. Students decide which words can't be changed and are most important.

3. Students decide which information can be combined or rearranged, as well as think of some alternative synonyms to use.

4. Students prepare their final paraphrase draft and then compare with another student or hand it in to the teacher.

Reverse Writing

Skills: Writing/reading

Time: 20 minutes

Level: Intermediate-advanced

Materials Required: Comprehension questions

Does this sound familiar? Students read a passage and then have to answer comprehension questions, either through writing or speaking with a partner. However, if you want to make things more interesting and challenge your students, consider doing this reverse writing activity.

Tell your students that you have comprehension questions but no reading passage. They can be anything you want, but here's one quick example:

- What was Tom's job?

- What was the weather like that day?

- What didn't he want to do? Why?

- What surprising thing happened at the end?

Get the students to be creative and answer the questions in point form. Then, they can write a short story about what happened to Tom. After that, each person can trade papers with another students who reads the story and sees if they can answer the comprehension questions. Finally, you can read the stories together as a class and vote on your favourite one.

Procedure:

1. Prepare some typical comprehension questions like you'd have for a short story. Give them to the students and tell them that you don't have the story but they'll need to make it up themselves.

2. Students answer the question in point form, and then write a short story.

3. Each student can trade with another student who reads the story and answers the original comprehension questions.

4. Read the stories out to the class and students can vote on their favourite one (optional).

Scrabble

Skills: Writing/reading

Time: 20+ minutes

Level: Intermediate-advanced

Materials Required: Oversized wall-mounted board, or one board per table and a set of letters

Your students will likely be familiar with Scrabble, either the board game or similar apps. It's a great way to get students to recall vocabulary and use correct spelling. It's a bit labor intensive to create the board(s) but I get several years of use out of a wall-mounted board.

To make a wall-mounted board, I use a large (big enough for letters to be seen across the classroom) piece of felt. Thin quilt batting is not as durable, but may be easier to come by. The Velcro on the back of the letters will pull bits of it off, but I still can get enough use out of a board to make it a viable option. I use an actual board as a guide for number of squares and arrangement of "special" squares, but I add in a few more than in the standard game. *Wikipedia* has the official list of number of letters and point value, which I use as well.

I make the letter cards about the size of my hand so that the words can be read across the classroom. I laminate them (of course!) and stick a square of "pointy" Velcro on the back. Since the board is felt or batting, the Velcro sticks right on.

If the class is lower-level, I have the students work in pairs or threes. If the class is quite large, I use table-top game boards. You can splurge and pay for real boards, but I just use A3 paper. I make a top board and bottom board, print them, cut off the border at the join, laminate them, and tape them together. You will need a set of letters of the appropriate size, but you don't need Velcro.

Procedure:

1. In advance, prepare one wall-mounted board with letter cards with Velcro on the back, or enough game boards and letter sets for each table to have one. (I use *Wikipedia* for the game board layout and letter point values and numbers.)

2. Depending on class size and level, have students work as individuals, pairs, or threes. (A large class playing as individuals on a wall-mounted board will create a lot of downtime.)

3. You may want to give bonuses for longer words. If necessary, start a new word in a corner of the board or add a long word of your own if there are a large number of 3-4 letter words.

Translation

Skills: Reading/writing

Time: Variable

Level: Intermediate-advanced

Materials Required: Passage to translate

Translating is often seen as kind of a dirty word in language learning (unless it is your intended career) but once students reach intermediate fluency, it can actually be useful. By this stage, they are probably pretty good at getting their point across on a variety of topics.

However, your students may find themselves becoming complacent. Since they can get their point across, they may not be as motivated to increase their vocabulary or use more complex grammatical structures. This is where translation can take writing to the next level.

When translating, you need to take the nuance of the original text into account. You aren't simply stating your ideas or opinions. You must choose the words which express the original meaning.

Procedure:

1. Choose a short article for your students to translate. Or they can choose their own.

2. Students read the article carefully and make a note of important words. Caution them against just starting with the first word and translating through to the end.

3. To start the translation, students just use those key words and phrases to recreate the article. As they practice more, they can work on being more exact.

4. Check the translations, or have students compare with other students. Rewrite the

corrected translation in a notebook.

But, Don't Translate Word for Word

I taught in South Korean universities for about 10 years. The best students were the ones who thought, talked, and wrote in English only. The weakest students were those that translated word for word between English and their first language. When you're listening, don't translate every single word into your first language. Listen to an entire sentence, or paragraph and then translate the main ideas, if necessary. Translating word for word is only helpful to remind you of how the same meaning is expressed differently between English and your first language.

Vocabulary Square

Skill: Writing

Time: 20+ minutes

Level: Intermediate

Materials Required: Index cards (students should be told in advance to bring one card per vocabulary word); dictionary or textbook with glossary

This is a class activity to facilitate self-study as well as dictionary skills. Many students these days rely on their electronic dictionaries for translations and don't develop their English-English dictionary skills. They may also not realize the benefits of flashcards for vocabulary self-study. Regular repetition of exposure to new words is necessary to commit them to working memory.

It is an easy activity to set up. Have students divide their index into four boxes by drawing a vertical and a horizontal line through the middle:

Box 1: Write the meaning in the student's own words.

Box 2: Write at least one synonym and one antonym.

49

Box 3: Write an example sentence.

Box 4: Draw an image representing the term.

Remind students to review the flashcards at least once a day.

Teaching Tips:

You may want to complete a few examples together to remind students to restate the definitions rather than copying them. A PowerPoint of a completed index card will help students more easily understand the task. You could also draw an example on the whiteboard.

Procedure:

1. At least one class in advance, ask students to bring index cards. Alternatively, you can cut copy paper into 8 pieces, but it is not as durable.

2. Explain to students that flashcards are a great way to learn new vocabulary if they review the cards often.

3. Have students divide their index cards into four corners, and fill as follows:

1. Write the meaning in the students' own words.

2. Write at least one synonym and one antonym.

3. Write an example sentence.

4. Draw an image representing the term.

Write an Email

Skills: Reading/writing

Time: 30+ minutes

Level: Intermediate-advanced

Materials Required: Example emails

Remember that writing is more than just a five-paragraph essay! It can include writing down some words in any form, whether long or short. So, why not get your students to work on writing an email in your class?

Email is quite a specific form of communication that has a few unwritten rules. If you follow them, the emails you send will be effective. If you don't, people probably won't read them!

The first tip I give my students is to keep emails brief, and direct. People get a lot of emails, especially at work. Make sure your emails are to the point! Make them very clear and easy to understand. Use simple grammar and vocabulary. The tone of your email should be polite, and not demanding.

Next, make sure you have a good subject line. By "good," we mean that it describes exactly what the email is about. For example, saying something like, "Hello friend," when your email is about an upcoming work meeting is bad! A better subject line would be, "Team A lunch meeting Jan. 2, 12:00."

Finally, don't forget to proofread. Read your email out loud at least once, checking for things like basic grammatical errors, spelling, etc.

Procedure:

1. Show students some example emails.

2. Give some tips about writing them. For example, choose a good subject line and keep it brief.

3. Give students a reason to write an email (upcoming work meeting, hosting a party, etc.) and they can write one. Check answers.

Writing Activities for Lower-Level Students

Here are some of my favourite activities for beginners or intermediates. The key thing to keep in mind is that ESL/EFL writing is more than just a 5-paragraph essay. It can even be as simple as filling in one word in a sentence.

Adjective or Adverb Modifier Posters

Skill: Writing

Time: 10-20 minutes

Level: Beginner-intermediate

Materials Required: A3 or butcher paper with a photo or two attached, one per group; markers

Optional Materials: Timer or buzzer

Students tend to have difficulty with correct adjective and adverb usage. This activity provides a chance to review them. In advance, prepare several images with a fair bit going on in them, such as people at a park engaged in different activities. Attach at least one image to each piece of paper. Each group of 3-5 students will need one piece of paper and at least one marker.

Begin with a review of adjectives and adverbs. Give and elicit examples until you feel the class is ready to complete the activity. Divide the class into groups of 3-4. Give each group one of the prepared pages and a set of markers. Have them write as many phrases describing the image(s) as they can which contain an adjective and/ or an adverb. They should then circle the adjectives and underline the adverbs.

Give a time limit of 5-10 minutes. If students mostly seem to be done before the time is up, go ahead and wrap up the activity. Time allowing, have each group display their paper and share their work with the class.

Teaching Tips:

To help students remember which is which, write on the board that they should circle adjectives and underline adverbs.

If you are going to have students display their work to the class, you might want to give more correction than usual as you mingle, to avoid embarrassment or shyness.

If you don't want to prepare images for each group, you can simply display one or two large images for the class to use.

Procedure:

1. In advance, prepare several images with a fair bit going on in them, such as people at a park engaged in different activities. Attach at least one image to each piece of A3 or butcher paper. (Each group of 3-5 students will need one piece of paper and at least one marker.)

2. Begin with a review of adjectives and adverbs. Give and elicit examples until you feel the class is ready to complete the activity.

3. Divide the class into groups of 3-4. Give each group one of the prepared pages and a set of markers.

4. Have them write as many phrases describing the image(s) as they can which contain an adjective and/or an adverb.

5. Have them circle the adjectives and underline the adverbs.

6. Give a time limit of 5-10 minutes. Time allowing, have each group display their paper and share their work with the class.

Alphabet Game

Skills: Writing

Time: 5 minutes

Level: Beginner

This is a simple way to introduce a topic. Some examples include jobs, cities, or animals. Have pairs of students write down A~Z on a piece of paper. Give them 2-4 minutes to think of one word per letter of the alphabet that falls within the category (e.g. animals). It's often very difficult to get a word for each letter in that time frame but the goal is to get as many as possible.

Here's an example of what students should NOT do:

A. alligator, ant, antelope

I make a rule that students can't use proper nouns. If you want to increase the difficulty or if you have a small class, you can make a rule that if two teams have the same word it doesn't count. This forces students to think more creatively, but it's too time-consuming to check this for bigger classes.

Example: topic = animals

A. alligator

B. bat

C. cat

Etc.

At the end, you can ask students to count how many words they got (remember only one for each letter). Then, check the top 1-3 teams, depending on how many prizes you have to give out! Or, if you have a very small class, you could easily check all the lists.

Procedure:

1. In pairs, students write down the alphabet on a piece of paper.

2. Give students a topic and a certain amount of time.

3. Students think of one word per alphabet letter about the topic.

4. Check who has the most letters completed at the end of the allotted time. Option for small classes: don't count repeated words so students have to think more creatively.

Correction Relay

Skill: Reading/writing

Time: 10+ minutes

Level: Beginner-intermediate

Materials Required: Worksheet

This is an activity that uses speed and competition to make something old (error correction) new again. Students of all levels should be quite familiar with finding and correcting errors in sentences. By adding a relay aspect, it will (hopefully) make an important but sometimes tedious skill new and more interesting.

To prepare the activity, create a worksheet with 10-15 errors. You can focus your errors on one aspect of vocabulary, such as synonyms and antonyms, or more simply, misuse vocabulary words in sentences. For lower level students, limit the errors to one per sentence. Higher levels can handle multiple errors in one sentence, and you can increase the challenge by having one vocabulary error per sentence and one or more other errors, such as grammar or punctuation mistakes.

The activity itself is straightforward. Students will work in teams of 4-5 to correct the worksheet as quickly as possible. Each student makes one correction and passes the worksheet to the next person who makes the next correction. They continue to pass the worksheet around until it is complete. You can make it easier by allowing students to choose any remaining sentence to correct, or you can require them to work from top to bottom.

Teaching Tips:

To prevent one student from carrying the rest of the team, do not allow other team members to correct another correction. That is, a sentence cannot be corrected by a second student once someone has corrected it. This also prevents more assertive (but not necessarily more able) students from incorrectly correcting others' work.

Also, to keep things moving along you may want to have a time limit for each turn before students must pass the worksheet along.

Procedure:

1. In advance, prepare a worksheet with 10-15 sentences containing vocabulary errors.

2. Divide students into groups of 4-5. If possible, group the desks to facilitate easy passing of the worksheets.

3. Have students take turns making one correction and passing the worksheet to the next student to make one correction. They continue passing and correcting until the worksheet is complete.

4. When all teams are finished, go over the errors as a class. The team with the most correct sentences wins.

Do you _____?

Skills: Writing/speaking/listening

Time: 15 minutes

Level: Beginner-intermediate

Materials Required: Strips of paper (or students can make their own)

Give each student five strips of paper. On each piece of paper they write something interesting about themselves. Then, collect them, mix them up and distribute them back to your students (three per student). At this point, everyone stands up and goes around the class asking questions to try to find the owner for each paper that they have. If someone is done early, you can give them another paper from the reserve pile that you have.

For example,

"Did you go to _____ middle school?"

"Do you have a twin brother?"

"Do you love to play soccer?"

Teaching Tip:

Students need to write down *interesting and unique* things about themselves. For example, "I go to XYZ university" is something that every other student in the class will say yes to so it is not a good thing to use.

Procedure:

1. Give students five strips of paper (or they provide their own).

2. Students write down one interesting thing about themselves on each paper.

3. Collect papers and redistribute (three per student).

4. Students stand up and go around the class, asking their classmates, "Do you have a twin brother?" "Can you play the piano really well?" based on what is on their papers.

5. If it's a match, they get one point and that paper is "finished." Optionally, you can require higher level students to ask 1-3 follow-up questions before they get a point.

6. If a student finds all their matches, they can get one or two more papers from your reserve pile.

-er Dictionary Activity

Skills: Reading/writing/speaking/listening

Time: 10+ minutes

Level: Intermediate

Materials Required: Worksheet

Students learn early on that –er refers to a person who does something. Examples include, teacher, writer, baker, etc. However, nouns ending in –er can refer to people, animals, or objects or can have multiple meanings involving a combination of the above. The activity will reinforce the need to be cautious with general rules in English while providing dictionary practice.

Begin by preparing a list of nouns ending with –er. If you would like this to be a brief activity, limit it to about five words. The more words you include, the longer the activity will be. Have three columns beside the list for students to tick if the word refers to a person, animal, and/or object. Students should use their dictionaries to determine which categories each word belongs to.

Here are enough –er words for an entire class period:

blender, bumper, buyer

cadaver, canister, cleaner, coaster, customer

diver, dozer, driver

fryer

hipster

oyster

passenger, pitcher, planner, player

ringer, roster

scanner, sticker, stinger

walker

To add a speaking element, have students work with partners after filling in their answers. Partners should take turns asking and answering questions about the words. For example, "A person who bakes is a baker. Is a person who cooks a cooker?"

Teaching Tip:

This may be a good time to review "a person who _____" and "a thing that _____."

Procedure:

1. In advance, prepare a worksheet with a list of nouns ending in –er with tick box columns for person, animal, and object. Also, at least one class beforehand, instruct students to bring their dictionaries on the appropriate date, if you do not have class sets.

2. Explain to students that although they know that nouns ending in –er are people, -er words can also refer to animals and objects.

3. Have students use their dictionaries to categorize each word on the list as person, animal, and/or object.

4. When students have looked up all the words, have them work with a partner asking and answering questions about the words. For example, "Is a walker a person who walks?" (Answer: "Yes, and also something that helps people walk.")

Give a Reason

Skill: Writing

Time: 5-10 minutes

Level: Beginner-intermediate

Materials Required: Nothing

If you're teaching your students about conjunctions, try out this simple activity. Write some sentence starters on the board using "because." For example:

- I was late for school because _____.

- My mom was angry at my sister because _____.

- I failed the test because _____.

Put students into pairs and they have to think of the most creative reasons they can to finish off the sentences. Compare answers as a class and choose the most interesting ones.

Teaching Tip:

This activity lends itself well to "so" sentences as well that deal with consequences. For example:

- I missed my bus so _____.

- I woke up late so _____.

Procedure:

1. Write some sentences on the board with "because," but leave the reason blank.

2. Put students into pairs and they have to creatively give the reason to finish the sentence.

3. Compare answers as a class.

Mixed Up Sentences

Skills: Reading/writing/speaking

Time: 5-10 minutes

Level: Beginner-intermediate

Materials Required: Nothing

Mixed up sentences is one of my favourite ways to review English grammar. I generally use it as a quick warm-up at the beginning of a class to review material from previous classes. It works well for beginner to intermediate level students of all ages. For advanced level students, it's far more difficult to make mixed up sentences without totally obvious mistakes that they'll pick up very, very easily.

For beginners and children, you may want to mix things up at the word level and have them make sentences by writing. However, for older, or more advanced level students, they can make a dialogue or story out of pre-made sentences.

Here's how to do it. Put up a "Mixed-Up" conversation or a few unrelated sentences on the board or in a PowerPoint presentation. The students then have to turn them into coherent English.

Teaching Tips:

If your goal is to practice specific grammar points, it will probably be faster to make your own dialogue or sentences than to repurpose one from the book.

However, if your students are beginners or high beginners, simply arranging a set of sentences in the correct order of a conversation may be challenging. In that case, you can save yourself some time by recycling a textbook dialogue which you covered several weeks or months earlier.

Procedure:

1. In advance, prepare a conversation using familiar vocabulary, or take a dialogue from a previous, but not too recent, lesson. Randomly arrange the sentences, or parts of sentences, if you want to make it more challenging.

For the highest level students, you could have them do both. First, arrange the sentences and then put them in some sort of order to make a coherent conversation.

2. Have students work in pairs or small groups to correctly arrange the sentences, or words within the sentences.

Q&A

Skills: Speaking/listening/reading/writing

Time: 10 minutes

Level: Beginner

Materials Required: Nothing

This is a simple variation on having students make example sentences using their vocabulary list. Students work in pairs of teams, creating a list of WH questions (to avoid yes/no answers) using their vocabulary words. When they have five questions, teams should alternate asking a question to another team and answering the other team's questions.

You can extend the activity with some reported speech practice, which will give teams an incentive to listen to the responses to their questions.

Procedure:

1. Divide students into an even number of teams of 2-4. Then pair two teams together.

2. Give students a few minutes to create five WH questions using their vocabulary words.

3. Have the paired teams alternate asking and answering each other's questions.

4. Optionally, extend the activity by having teams briefly report the other team's answers.

Synonym/Antonym Brainstorm Race

Skill: Writing

Time: 5 minutes

Level: Intermediate

Materials Required: Large paper (one piece per group) or whiteboard and markers (at least one per group)

This is a nice activity to use with new vocabulary, after introducing the terms and definitions. To play, divide students into groups of 4-5 and give each group at least one marker. If you are not using the whiteboard, also give each group one piece of A3 or butcher paper. Give students a time limit of 2-3 minutes to list all of the vocabulary words they can remember from the previous lesson. With higher-level classes, have students add a synonym, antonym, or brief definition. The group with the most correct words wins.

Procedure:

1. In advance, prepare markers and optionally, a piece of A3 or butcher paper for each group.

2. Divide students into groups of 4-5.

3. Have students work together to list all of the vocabulary and add at least one synonym and antonym of each word.

4. The group with the most correct words wins.

What's That Called?

Skill: Writing/reading

Time: 5-10 minutes

Level: Beginner

Materials Required: Package of Post-It notes

If you're teaching about classroom vocabulary, then try out this fun activity. Give each student a few Post-It notes and have them walk around the classroom, labelling common objects (clock, chair, textbook, table, etc.). Students will have a pen or pencil in their hand so emphasize that it's walking only and it's not a race to see who can get the most objects!

When you run out of Post-It notes, or most things are labelled, have students sit down. Then, walk around the class and review students' labels to ensure they're correct. Pick them up as you go.

When you have all the labels, mix them up and redistribute them back to the students who must put the labels on the objects as a kind of review.

Procedure:

1. Give each student a few Post-It notes. They will take their pencil and walk around the class, labelling the objects.

2. When they're done, check and see if their labels are correct. Collect the papers as you go.

3. Redistribute the papers back to the students who must put the labels on the objects one more time.

What's the Question?

Skill: Writing/listening

Time: 10 minutes

Level: Beginner-intermediate

Materials Required: Nothing

This is a fun whiteboard game that you can play with everyone but very advanced students (it will be too easy for them). Put students into two, three or four teams. The number of teams will depend on the size of your class and whiteboard, but the more teams the better. A greater number of teams is more student-centered, but you'll have to have a larger whiteboard because everyone needs space to write on it.

Then, say the answer to some question. The difficulty depends on the general level of the class. Students have to write a possible question that corresponds with your answer. The first person to do it gets a point for their team. Continue the game until everyone has had a chance, or the time is up.

Here are some beginner examples, with a possible answer in brackets:

- My name is Jackie. (What's your name?)

- It's sunny. (How's the weather?)

- It's behind me. (Where's the clock?)

Note that there may be more than one answer for some questions. You will have to use your discretion.

Procedure:

1. Put students into teams and have one student from each come up to the whiteboard.

2. Say an answer to a question and students race to see who can write the question first.

3. The first person who is correct gets a point for their team.

4. Continue until everyone has had a chance to play.

What Can Students Write About?

Are you at a bit of a loss for what your students can write about in your class? There are a ton of ideas, including a short story, picture, life story, hopes for the future and more. Here are more details about each of these things.

A Short Story

For something different, try writing a short fiction story. Think of an idea and start writing! You can write a story for children, teens, or adults. Let your creativity take over. Remember to build some suspense, and of course, include a good hook at the beginning so that people will want to keep reading it. Don't worry so much about following any certain writing style, or structure. There's a lot of freedom when writing a fiction story.

To make it more interesting, don't use boring words. Check out this handout I give my students filled with descriptive words: www.jackiebolen/words.

A Picture

If you aren't sure what to write about, use a picture. This can be a photo you have taken, one from the Internet or newspaper, or a work of art. You can use it for descriptive writing or as a prompt for creative writing. Here are some questions to get you started:

- What can you see in the picture?

- Are there people? What are they doing? Look at their faces. Happy, sad, angry . . .

- What is the setting? In a house, at a beach, on a city street . . .

- How is the weather?

- What is happening? If you don't know, get creative!

Life Story

It can be good practice to write your life story. This will require you to write using past tense verbs almost entirely. If you need a quick review of past tense verbs, you can check this out (http://www.englishpage.com/verbpage/simplepast.html). For your story, you can start at the very beginning, and go up to the present time, talking about the highlights. Or, you can focus on a specific period in time such as middle school. Another way to write about the past is choose an interesting story, and write specifically about that. Just remember to pay special attention to the verbs!

Hopes for the Future

It can also be good practice to write about the future. This will require you to use future tense verbs. If you're a little unsure about when to use a certain future verb tense, give yourself a quick test (http://www.englishlessonsbrighton.co.uk/future-tenses-exercise/) and see how you do! Once you have the basics of the future tense down, write about your hopes for the future. You can answer the question, "Where do you see yourself in 10 years?"

Forums

No matter what your hobbies or interests are, there are online forums for people with the same interests. Search for some English-language groups focused on topics you are interested in. Simply *Google* (topic)+forum. If the results are in your own language, make sure you are on google.com, rather than your home country. Posts should be related to the group topic, so you are more likely to know or want to know the vocabulary. Posts are also usually quite short, so you won't get overwhelmed by a wall of text. You also shouldn't feel pressure to write a long post.

Facebook Groups

If you would rather use *Facebook* than join another website, don't worry; there are thousands of groups for every interest you can imagine. You may need to change your *Facebook* language to English to get the search results you want. As on forums, *Facebook* posts are usually short, so you won't feel pressure to write a lot. You don't even have to write anything at all until you feel comfortable participating.

Twitter

Twitter is a fun way to practice English writing. Sign-up for a free account and follow some people. Hopefully they will follow you back. You can search for something like, "ESL," or "learn English" to find other English learners like yourself.

Journaling

If you're not in the habit of journaling, it can be a little bit difficult at the beginning. But, start slowly with 4 or 5 sentences per day. You can gradually increase the sentences to 10 or more. Then just keep doing it at least 4 or 5 days a week. Writing every day is best. It gets easier over time and your writing and speaking will both improve.

If you want someone to correct your writing, check out Lang-8. This is a community of native speakers and language learners who correct each other's writing. The catch is, you have to correct someone's writing before you get your writing corrected. The more you help others, the more help you can receive.

Describe a Scene

One problem with practicing writing is that it is often difficult to think of a topic. Many people keep a journal, but if every day you write about the same activities and experiences, you will not improve. This is one idea which will give you endless material to write. Sources of scenes to describe include photos, paintings, TV shows, and movies.

You can simply describe what you see (or picture in your mind, if describing a scene from a book or creating an imaginary scene). To describe a scene from a TV show or movie, imagine you are explaining it to a blind person. If you want more of a challenge, write a story based on a photo or painting. Ask yourself:

Who are the people?

What are they doing?

What emotions are they feeling?

Add sensory details about the sights, sounds, smells, etc. you can see or imagine from the image.

Short Writing Activities for Beginners

Do you want to direct your students to some of the best online resources? Here are some of my favourites.

If you are a beginner at writing in English, or just want to review the basics, then check out this list:

http://esl.fis.edu/learners/writing/misc/index_color.htm

There are 72 simple exercises. Use the "checklist" to keep track of which ones you have done.

Stickyball.net

Similar to the website mentioned above, *Stickyball.net* has a lot of resources for beginner writers. Check out this link: http://www.stickyball.net/esl-writing-exercises-and-activities.html. They are mostly for beginners, but could be a good way to review the basics such as error correction and sentence patterns.

BBC Skillwise

There are some excellent activities for English learners at this website. Here is the link to the writing ones: http://www.bbc.co.uk/skillswise/topic-group/writing. They are a bit more advanced level than the previous websites mentioned and cover things like formatting and style, writing a letter and handwriting.

Get a Pen Pal

If you can coordinate it, pen pals are a very interesting way for students to practice their writing. You can try finding a teacher in another country with similar age students on some of the English teacher *Facebook* groups or forums. Or, your students could find their own pen-pal. More details about this in the next paragraph.

Sites like *Pen Pal World* and *Global Pen Friends* let you search for pen pals all over the world. This is a bit different than the other suggestions because you will just be writing to one another socially. Your pen pal will not be a tutor, study buddy, or language exchange partner. You improve your writing as you communicate with your pen pal who may or may not be a native English speaker. On the other hand, *InterPals* is a site just for language learners looking for language exchange partners. You enter which language you speak and which language you want to study.

You could consider offering this option as a way for students to get bonus points in your class. I've never done it, but have often thought that it'd be a nice option!

Blogging

One way that students can improve their writing and speaking is to start a blog. They can share their ideas, thoughts and daily life with the world. Some of the best free platforms include: *Blogger*, *Tumblr* and *Wordpress*.

Encourage students to share what they post with their friends and family on *Facebook, Twitter, Pinterest* or other social media channels. Encourage the students in the class to comment on each other's blogs with their own thoughts.

Students can also record some short videos and post them on their blog. They'll get better at speaking by practicing speaking, but they'll also get better at writing by preparing an outline (or full script) for their video!

I used to teach university students in South Korea and I assigned videos to my students for homework. Many of the students didn't like it at the time because they were shy. However, at the end of the course, they said it was one of the most useful things they did.

There are various ways that you can get your students blogging. If you have access to a computer lab, you may want to get students doing it during class time. But, set a requirement such as they must complete one blog post with a minimum of 100 words and comment on two other class blogs during that class time. Or, complete it for homework.

Another option is to have students write a certain number of articles as a homework assignment. I've often given my students the option of either journaling in a notebook or doing an online blog. A surprising number chose the blog option!

Before You Go

If you found this book useful, please head on over to *Amazon* and leave a review. It will help other teachers find the book. Also be sure to check out my other books on *Amazon*: www.amazon.com/author/jackiebolen. There are plenty more ESL activities and games for children as well as adults. Here are some of the most popular titles:

39 No-Prep/Low-Prep ESL Speaking Activities

39 ESL Icebreakers

39 Awesome 1-1 ESL Activities

101 ESL Activities

Life After ESL: Foreign Teachers Returning Home

Made in the USA
Middletown, DE
05 February 2024

49158829R00045